How
to Have
a Giving Church

Bartlett L. Hess
and
Margaret Johnston Hess

Abingdon Press   Nashville   New York

HOW TO HAVE A GIVING CHURCH

Copyright © 1974 by Abingdon Press

Library of Congress Cataloging in Publication Data

Hess, Bartlett L.   1910-   How to have a giving church.

1. Christian giving. 2. Church finance.
I. Hess, Margaret Johnston, joint author. II. Title.
BV772.H45   254.8   74-6186

ISBN 0-687-17808-8

Scripture quotation noted Beck is from The New Testament
in the Language of Today © copyright 1963 by Concordia
Publishing House.

Scripture quotations noted RSV are from the Revised Standard
Version of the Bible. Copyrighted 1946, 1952, and 1971 by
the Division of Christian Education, National Council of
Churches, and are used by permission.

Scripture quotations noted NEB are from The New English
Bible © the Delegates of the Oxford University Press, and
the Syndics of the Cambridge University Press 1961, 1970.

Scripture quotations noted LB are from The Way, by the
editors of *Campus Life Magazine,* copyright © 1971 by
Tyndale House Publishers.

Scripture quotation noted Phillips is from The New Testament
in Modern English, copyright 1958 by J. B. Phillips.

MANUFACTURED BY THE PARTHENON PRESS AT
NASHVILLE, TENNESSEE, UNITED STATES OF AMERICA

To

---

the many people in our churches
who joined hearts and hands with us.
They made this story possible.

We wish to express appreciation to
Mrs. Marilynn Adams for patience and skill
in typing, retyping our manuscript.

Contents

HOW TO HAVE A GIVING CHURCH

Prologue

"Like a mighty army moves the Church of God."
But if the church doesn't have enough dollars,
it doesn't move far.

None of us likes to have money extracted from
us forcibly; we don't like pressure tactics. But,
a pastor can bring his people into touch with
spiritual principles of giving. The Holy Spirit can
make us *want* to give. Then the church has the
money it needs, our lives have a new dimension
of joy in giving.

How? What are these principles? Together my
husband and I have prayed, searched, and gradually discovered principles of giving that work for
us. Our experiences have been in small, medium,

and large congregations where he has been the pastor. My viewpoint is that of the person in the pew—I know what people will take and what they won't take.

Results have been beyond our dreams.

Sharing the Needs

"What do these fellows have that I don't have?" asked Bart gloomily. He was studying our denominational records of individual churches. We were in our first little church, and he was having trouble raising the $4,000 that comprised the entire yearly budget.

I had no suggestions to offer though I had grown up in a manse. Money for the church to me was like the dark currents of the ocean. It was something that mysteriously flowed toward some people and away from others. In my childhood home the semiannual interest payments on the building debt were recurring crises. In this church that Bart served just out of seminary, the big problem was how to meet the coal bill.

One day he came home jubilant. He had had

lunch with a friend, a peer in a comparable church, who had no problem with money.

"Ray says the secret of raising money is sharing problems with the congregation. You share money problems with your family—the church is a family. He says don't keep still about money, but don't nag, scold, beg, or plead. Simply share needs, and people will respond."

Bart tried it and it worked. It was spring; the coal bill had not yet been paid. Bart shared the problem with the congregation comprised mostly of working people.

Before the offering one Sunday he said, "We have an unpaid coal bill of $390 from last winter, and we need to pay the coal man. Perhaps you have some of the Lord's money you would like to contribute to clear this up. The Bible instructs us, 'Owe no one anything, except to love one another'" (Romans 13:8 RSV).

After a Sunday or two the whole bill was paid. Those people could see the problem—the man who had furnished them with coal all winter deserved to be paid.

Bart and I were thrilled. We decided to hold a "Rejoicing Sunday" to share the good news. Never before had we had anything financial to rejoice about in that church. It was a complete change of pace. We sent out cards; people poured out for thanksgiving in April. In a family you share good things as well as bad.

Actually, sharing is a very minor facet of our total program for giving. But it was the first thing we learned, and it's a good place to start. It takes a while to get the hang of it completely, and we stumbled a number of times.

What and how do you share? You don't share every little need that comes along. Nobody wants a church service to sound like a financial meeting. You do share any emergency in the church. Or perhaps a world emergency is on everyone's mind —typhoon in India, earthquake in Peru. You can offer a chance to share in relief.

Or, you share a special need on the mission field you've just learned about. Some missionary's car has broken down, he simply can't carry on. Or a medical emergency has struck his family.

You share positively as well as negatively. If you are putting up a new building, keep people informed on progress. State in the bulletin or church paper whether income is keeping pace with costs. Don't hide bad news.

Share what is being done with money already given. If you are supporting a worker in the inner city, let him tell about his work. Instruct him not to ask for a special offering. He's to let people know what he's accomplishing with dollars already given.

Let a young person tell what the church has meant in his or her life. You can mention that dollars already given are supporting the youth program.

If a missionary supported by your church can visit, feature him. Instruct him to tell what he is doing, not to make a pitch for money. As people give more, you may be able to increase his allotment in the coming year.

At all times, share with church members what is going on. All missionary programs at home and abroad and their progress are their affair.

What? Your giving has increased beyond your budget? That has happened to us many times. Board members always think that is the time to keep still. They're afraid people will stop giving. Not at all. Rejoice! Proclaim it! Let people know what their extra dollars are doing. There is no such thing as too much money for the church. You can always give it away.

Should the Minister Talk About Money?

Ministers don't offer their congregations lessons in giving for various reasons. We didn't, because we didn't know how. Seminaries don't teach you this. We had to learn it the hard way—trial and error.

Most ministers are happy to accept raises but can't figure out where they come from. Other ministers feel they alone can balance a wobbling budget by cutting their personal needs to the bone.

Simon Self-Sacrifice, of course, renounced dreams of riches when he entered the ministry. He believes his responsibility is to preach the gospel, tend the sick, care for the poor. He feels it's up to his congregation to provide him with worldly goods. They are to decide what he needs to sustain life on this planet.

They do. They give him a salary that equals whatever is left after all bills are paid. Obviously, they couldn't live on so little. But they assume a minister has some mysterious way of multiplying dollars and cents—and he does. He makes his calls in a ramshackle car that breaks down frequently. He can't afford repair bills, so he spends hours tinkering with the car himself. He paints his own house, keeps a garden, helps can vegetables. He washes windows, attempts his own plumbing repairs, and then can't understand where all his time goes.

Naturally, Simon Self-Sacrifice can't afford many books. Books at the library are fine, but they're never on hand when he's preparing Sunday's sermon. When he has a few minutes to relax, there are no new magazines to pick up. Magazines, like books, cost money.

Everybody loves Simon Self-Sacrifice. But they don't much care about listening to him preach. They don't bring friends to church. They don't ask him to call on new neighbors. They're a little bit ashamed of how he looks, the kind of car he drives, the stale sound of his preaching. They wish he would realize that a certain style is required in their kind of neighborhood.

There is quite a case, of course, for Simon to have an adequate salary. But he's a little mixed up. He doesn't realize what the Bible says about needs. "And my God will supply every need of yours according to his riches in glory in Christ Jesus" (Philippians 4:19 RSV).

Our denomination doesn't pay salaries to ministers of course. That would seem too crass. But they do extend written calls promising to provide a certain sum of money per annum. This money is to make the minister free of worldly cares and avocations. Puttering over cars, pipes, and paint pails would for most ministers constitute worldly cares and avocations. He could better use his time.

Simon has failed to convey to his congregation God's plan for caring for ministers. God normally doesn't waft his riches directly from glory. He has given simple instructions in his Word: "Pastors who do their work well should be paid well and should be highly appreciated, especially those who work hard at both preaching and teaching. For the scriptures say, 'Never tie up the mouth of an ox when it is treading out the grain—let him eat as he goes along!' And in another place, 'Those who work deserve their pay!' " (I Timothy 5:17-18 LB).

Like the ox, the minister has to eat. For greatest efficiency he should have enough money to feed himself well. A high protein, vitamin-rich diet is supposed to work best for other people. Why not for him? He should be able to buy books and have time-consuming jobs done *for* him.

But here's a word of caution for Simon. There is absolutely no use in telling his financial board he needs more money. They haven't the faintest idea of how to bring in more money. They might be only too happy to give him more if it were there. Simon must realize it's his responsibility to teach his congregation to give.

Some ministers don't educate in financial stewardship because they think that's the trustees' job. That, of course, sounds like a nice idea. But we've never known it to work. Trustees simply aren't in a position to educate whole congregations. All they can do is approach individuals. As we'll learn later on, that's wrong. Boards can help, but the minister must assume leadership in the area of giving.

Perhaps most ministers don't talk about money because they're afraid people will object. In this case, the best defense is a good offense. Search the scriptures. What does the Bible say about the pastor's responsibility in teaching people to give?

Don't Nag or Scold

In sharing, keep special appeals down to a minimum. Norman Nagger has no problem about keeping silent on the subject of money. He is absolutely convinced people ought to give, and he is not afraid to stand up in the pulpit and say so. Nor does he falter at approaching people in their homes for special gifts. He trembles not at talking to his boards about needs large or small.

Of course he has an annual every-member canvass. And that is only the beginning. Next he hits his members with little folders into which they put a dime every month. Then these folders are sent to the poor orphans in Afghanistan, or the inner city, or any place to get them out of the house.

Beyond the dimes every month, ladies hit other

ladies with a butterfly coffee. Such affairs used to be known as silver teas. The ladies all got together to listen to silver dropping into a little dish. It was for Sister Miranda on the mission field. Now they don't want to hear any money dropping, but the idea is the same.

Modern women don't want to sit around listening to money either drop or float. They have already made a pledge to the church that's supposed to cover everything. What does the board do with all that money? Reportedly they give some to missions.

But, along comes Donald Do-gooder with his special project. He wants everyone to sign one of his little cards for $1,000. He feels a school for chicken-raising in Mozambique would straighten out the world's problems.

Norman Nagger gladly opens his pulpit to Silas Scarface. His job is to go around tossing boomerangs into congregations. It's not his fault if people leap to support his special project of churches in Chile. Later he'll come back to say they failed to meet their regular quota for missions. Norman needs to protect Silas against himself. He doesn't need any more of those scars on his face from appeals that boomerang.

The Reverend Mr. Scarface fades from the scene. Then the church board discovers an oversight—they didn't include money in the budget to repair the typewriters. So, they run a special campaign and have a committee buy two new typewriters. The office staff is happy, and the congregation feel they have done something.

But then the Reverend Mr. Nagger presents another special project. The choir needs new robes. But people now are getting tone-deaf. And by the time every-member canvass rolls around once again, they're stone deaf. The campaign falls flat.

So what can you do the next year except have a lot of special little projects? You have to get the bills paid and give something at least to missions. What Mr. Nagger hasn't heard about is that he must learn to carry all his begs in one ask-it.

When I was starting out as a mother, my mother-in-law gave me a pointer. "The trouble with nagging," she said, "is that children soon don't hear what you say. You must say a thing *once* to a child, then expect him to do it."

I thought nagging was bad just because everybody wants to stay away from a nagger. I learned from her that nagging is bad because it doesn't work.

Paul the apostle knew of a way to avoid nagging. "On the first day of every week, each of you is to put something aside and store it up, . . . so that contributions need not be made when I come" (I Corinthians 16:2 RSV).

Paul figured out the need ahead of time and told people to be ready for it. These days they call that making out a budget.

Also the trouble with nagging is it quite easily leads to scolding because the present need seems so terribly urgent. For instance, the choir director delivered an ultimatum. He said he'd quit if he didn't have new choir robes for the Christmas concert. Norman really had to scold to get them.

Of course nobody wants to be around a scolder. That's why they all cut out when it came to the every-member canvass. They got caught on the choir robes, though, and after that things went from bad to worse. Norman called up the finance chairman the next day. He scolded him because the canvass had flopped. The finance chairman scolded the session at the next board meeting. He said they should set the pace in giving. Board members scolded the congregation for being so stingy. The congregation scolded (i.e., criticized) the minister. Each person thought the minister should be able to get money out of other people.

Scolding, like typhoid, is contagious. Pretty soon Norman had to go to another church. There, alas, the same pattern repeated itself.

All this was for want of Norman's understanding the biblical basis for giving. "Each one must do as he has made up his mind, not reluctantly or under compulsion, for God loves a cheerful giver" (II Corinthians 9:7 RSV).

Do you see yourself in Norman Nagger? If so, find another image.

Don't Beg

There's a narrow border between sharing and begging. Sharing puts the other person on your own level. You're opening up to him some privileged information. You're including him as a member of the family. You're giving him a chance to be part of something important.

On the other hand, a beggar succeeds because he takes a stance below those whose pity he hopes to stir. He looks ragged, blind, crippled. He must appear unable to function. You may drop something into the cup of a beggar on the street. But you have a feeling of revulsion as you do it. You ask yourself questions. The next time you may walk on the other side of that street.

Byron Beggar lets people know his church is practically in a wheelchair. He looks as pitiful as possible—the better to get a few crumbs of support. He announces the electricity will soon be shut off, the roof is leaking. He himself is a month and a half behind in his salary. His wife works in a dime store to make ends meet.

Byron has a lean and hungry look that bothers people. They feel he thinks too much—about their fur coats, pounds of flesh, Buick sedans. He asks them to deprive themselves of that extra piece of pie. He begs them to rescue the church from bankruptcy.

They know an extra piece of pie is not going to rescue the church from bankruptcy. But they do what he asks—drop in an extra quarter. He asks for a pittance, that's exactly what he gets. And the next Sunday they will stay at home to make their car payments in peace.

The trouble with Byron is he thinks he's asking for charity. He's too diffident. He feels he has no claim to hard cash for nonmaterial, spiritual goods. He wouldn't say that in so many words, of course; but he really feels like a leech on the community. He doesn't produce bolts, bushels of wheat, or bank statements. These things are popularly viewed as tangible goods. People view the church's operations as intangible. It's easy to feel intangible goods shouldn't have to be paid for.

Byron is sincere. He believes in what he's doing. But his tone says he is asking for something to which he has no claim. (Sometimes the only difference between begging and sharing is the tone of voice.) Byron has forgotten he serves the Lord of the universe. Bolts, bushels of wheat, and bank statements are baby stuff.

God created morning stars that sing together. He created the springs of the sea and the dwelling place of light. He flung those stars into the heavens just for fingerwork. He made the earth. He allotted to man a little space and time to work within his creation. And you should *beg* puny man to drop a few coins into an offering plate? For shame! Get up out of that wheelchair, and walk in the power of Christ! No amount of earnestness or insistence will make up for taking the wrong stance.

You are not asking for something to which you have no claim or right. God owns the whole thing. He lets men manage little parts of his estate for a while. Your job as pastor? To acquaint man with the fair share he owes God. It's a small portion to be returned for all benefits received.

Don't Plead

The trouble with pleading is it's a one-shot deal. It's your day in court. A lawyer before a jury may use arguments, evidence, and sob stories. He pulls out all the stops. He wants the decision to go his way today. Tomorrow the jury will be dismissed, and he'll be on a different case. But not you. You'll be facing the same congregation next week —and next year you hope.

Pleading is the method used by most direct-mail requests for money. Where do most of these appeals go? Into the waste basket. You just can't take in that much horror. However, Peter Pleader has some real people sitting before him. He is under terrible pressure. A new church building has the foundation laid and the steel girders up.

Money for the building fund this month has not come in. The bills are $12,433.00; receipts are only $7,960.79.

Peter had pulled out all the stops before to get the pledges. Now people are not keeping up with their payments. He argues against their silent claim that they don't need a new church. They sit there like cabbage heads while he shreds them up. He says it's too late to back out now. Foundations and steel girders won't do anyone any good. The only way out is onward. He tells tear-jerking stories of churches never finished. He describes half-built walls, beams piercing the sky—monuments to lack of faith.

His members are good people. They don't want the town to laugh because they didn't count the cost before starting. They come up with money needed, and the building goes on to completion. Next year, however, they cut their pledges to missions and operating expenses.

Here's the "Peter Principle for Pleading": Giving, expanded by pressure, is money borrowed from the future. You can widen a stream into a pond any time you want to. But the flow below the pond will be greatly reduced for some time to come. You may even have a dry stream bed. A sounder way to widen a stream? Bring in more tributaries or increase the rainfall. Increasing the rainfall means getting in touch with the source.

In giving, the source is "as God hath prospered him" (I Corinthians 16:2). That means giving is to be in proportion to what the *person has*. It is not in proportion to what the *church needs*.

Foundation for Giving

For us, sharing worked so well that every Sunday was a rejoicing Sunday. Each week the bulletin carried a statement of favorable balance in the treasury. The church was a poor little inner city work, considered a mission until recently. Self-maintenance restored respect. A favorable balance put on a new roof, painted the walls, bought new drapes. Missionary giving mounted.

The following spring, a committee from a vacant church sat in the congregation. After the service, they expressed intrigue with the financial statement in the bulletin. Money was their chief problem; they couldn't meet their building interest payments. Those few thought they would like to have Bart as their pastor. He knew all about their church and had stated categorically, to me, his opinion of it. It was one of two churches he would never consider going to.

But the committee were such nice people. Bart didn't have the heart to say no right off. Besides, we believed Proverbs 3:5-6. "Trust in the Lord with all thine heart; and lean not unto thine own understanding. In all thy ways acknowledge him, and he shall direct thy paths." So there was one proper thing to do—go through the motions of having an open mind. Bart did.

He talked to them about their program. Their entire women's program consisted of money-raising schemes. They cooked suppers for money. They worked all year on a bazaar. They sold tickets to plays. They collected contributions from neighbors and business people. The entire Sunday evening program consisted of dancing to a jukebox. The officers believed it good to keep young people off the streets.

On Sunday mornings about twenty-five people worshiped in Gothic beauty.

Bart pointed out they lacked what he considered the whole foundation for giving. They wouldn't want him for a pastor because they would have to change everything. They would have to give up all money-raising schemes. They would have to accommodate themselves to biblical preaching. They would have to accept education in tithing, give their money directly. They would have to agree to attend prayer meetings, Bible classes, mission study. They would have to discontinue their present Sunday-evening programs. They would have to teach the Bible throughout the Sunday school. In short, they would have to have a spiritual program.

They disappeared for a few weeks. We talked and appreciated our poor little church anew. It was getting squared around to the point where it was good to be there. We realized that with all it lacked in opportunity, it had the foundation for giving. It had had seventy-five years of spiritual ministry. That was why the sharing concept had worked like instant magic. All prerequisites were present. We agreed we would rather stay where we were than take on impossible problems.

A few Sundays later a larger committee presented itself from the same church. They said they had talked it all over and decided to try religion. All agreed they had already tried everything else to keep the church going, but nothing had worked. They asked Bart to please come and preach in their church to be voted on as pastor.

Bart was shocked. He had never expected to see them again. He said he would have to think it over.

I watched him ease into the channel that would take him to the locks. We began to feel God's finger on us, nudging us along. I watched him jitter, pray, groan, hope. He was a young man with large ambitions and many degrees. He had great dreams of excellence for Christ. However, he agreed to preach. He was sure after they had heard him preach, they would know he didn't fit. He didn't know a woman in that church was praying specifically for a spiritual church. He would fit.

He still didn't want to go. We decided to put out the fleece. Bart would lay out very specifically all the changes he wanted. Undoubtedly these changes wouldn't be accepted, but he would have given God a chance.

All organizations accepted all changes. They voted they wanted him as pastor. He was to come to a congregational meeting to accept the call. Also, they wanted to talk further about the new program. He asked for one final vote at the meeting after he had made it all absolutely clear.

We were getting dressed to go to the meeting.

"What'll I do if they vote to accept all my conditions?"

"What can you do?" I asked. "You'll have to accept the call."

Maybe fifty people were present at the meeting.

He talked. They voted. He accepted.

The woman who had prayed rushed to the piano and began pounding out, "Praise God from whom all blessings flow." She told us later she had been up at three o'clock that morning praying for this meeting.

It was a tearful moment. We now had a church of fifty (for sure) lovable people. We also had a building debt of $80,000.

The locks had closed on us. They would carry us either up or down.

How Do You Build a Foundation?

If you have ever altered a house drastically, you know how costly changes can be. Sometimes it's cheaper to tear it all down and start over.

Sometimes you are in a position to do that in a church, as we were. We certainly recommend it. Going to that new church we felt like Columbus sailing an uncharted sea. We felt we might drop off the edge of the world. However, we were very sure God had called us to the task. And we believe what he asks us to do he will enable us to accomplish.

Impossible as such a complete change sounds, those people accepted it wholeheartedly. Perhaps the abruptness had shock value. They were profoundly relieved. They could stop performing all kinds of unpleasant duties. They no longer had to badger their neighbors to buy tickets for their church. Women could stop cooking suppers for money. They could stop asking merchants to give things to sell at their bazaar.

To that burdened congregation, straight-out giving seemed brilliant in its functional simplicity. They watched in mystic wonderment this miracle that was going to be wrought. It hadn't really occurred to them that they were going to do the giving.

With the courage of youth, we had cut off practically all previous sources of income. Yet, staggering payments on the building debt came due with shattering regularity. Those payments were like the great swinging balls used for pounding condemned buildings to pieces. Payments would have to be met before they struck. Practically no one had any training or background in giving. There was no habit of direct support of the church, no background in the Bible.

Sitting in the pew, I pondered the problem. People had to be made to *want* to do what we wanted them to. We wanted them to give. We knew we couldn't nag, scold, beg, or plead for money. We could only *share*. A whole viewpoint and sense of responsibility had to be built up.

We concentrated on building foundations, while starting education in giving. We considered sharing the good news of the gospel to be the absolute bottommost pilings. A very young church, they had thought a beautiful building would bring in the people. It didn't.

Biblical preaching was new to them. They liked it. It spoke to their hearts. As church members came to know Christ, they asked, "Why didn't someone tell us this before?" (Perhaps someone had—but they hadn't understood.) Now they were profoundly grateful. Never once did anyone ever say to us we should go back to the old way. A few left, but they left silently. We had not duped or hoodwinked anyone into anything. The old program had been voted down. It was all fair and square.

Perhaps the hardest thing for them to relinquish was the annual bazaar. That was the peak of the year socially and financially. We proposed a Harvest Home Dinner instead—turkey and all the trimmings. They were to sell no tickets, set no price. Good music and an outstanding speaker would constitute the program. Bart suggested that each person give a day's pay. This struck them as an easy substitute for all the work of a bazaar.

The women handled the change graciously. Before we arrived, they all got together. They sold each other the things they had been making for the bazaar.

In November, men and women cooperated to produce a delicious meal. Fellowship Hall was full of people, the atmosphere festive. They brought their offerings in envelopes. No one was excluded on the basis of money. Afterwards they counted up the offering. It was $525. The most they had ever made from a bazaar was $350. Many sat around late marveling and rejoicing.

It was the end of bazaars and all money-raising schemes.

Is Stewardship
the Minister's Job?

In weaker moments all ministers dream of:

(1) A church heavily endowed so they can concentrate on more important things than money.

(2) A church where officers take responsibility for money-raising.

(3) Some fairy godparent who will make up all deficits.

The trouble with (1) is all too often an endowed church is a dead church. (Human nature is what it is.) It's good for a minister to have to set forth his product in saleable form. If he doesn't, his mornings may shrink to an hour or two. His afternoons may shrivel to a call or two. His evenings may become a time to rest up.

Viewing the fjords of Norway from a boat deck one summer, we fell into conversation. Our Norwegian friend seemed eager to talk. "The only living churches in Norway," he said, "are the little self-supporting ones. We belong to one of those. The state churches are dead. Ministers get their salary whether anyone attends or not. I have been at services with only nine people present in a great cathedral."

Said a doctor to me, "One advantage I had as a child which I can't give my children is poverty. I had to work."

Paul said, "Not because I desire a gift; but I desire fruit that may abound to your account" (Philippians 4:17).

Strange as it seems, the Bible knows us better than we know ourselves. It says Christians need the spiritual exercise of giving. "For where your treasure is, there will your heart be also" (Matthew 6:21). And ministers benefit from the spiritual challenge of teaching people to give.

We all know of heavily endowed downtown churches. The endowment doesn't necessarily solve their problems, it may stunt growth in giving and participating. Do you dare set your child in an easy chair and give him everything?

The trouble with (2) is church officers generally can only carry out mechanics. In money-raising many can do a bang-up job of running a pledge campaign. But those exercises are least important in the whole operation. Officers generally cannot deepen the channel of giving by education. They cannot broaden it by spiritual growth. That the minister must do as spiritual leader.

One trouble with (3) is that fairy godparents are scarce. Potential ones usually lack (a) the ability, or (b) the inclination. Bart and I have known a lot of churches intimately. (He too was a child of the manse.) Neither of us has ever touched a real benefactor who made up all deficits. We've both known about such churches— secondhand. Bart always made sure the knowledge stayed secondhand. Such benefactions usually have a price tag attached. So you might let somebody, like us, help lift the load onto *your* shoulders. Happily you'll find you can carry it quite easily.

One summer day we were hiking an easy trail with a ranger in the Tetons. A man in the group told us he was used to scaling peaks. His forays into the mountains of course required a backpack. Someone always helped him lift his load and adjust it, he said. He could easily carry all day a load he couldn't even lift from the ground.

You think you can't take on the burden of finances? Remember, carrying it is all in getting the balance right. Your job is not the mechanics. Your job is teaching the spiritual basis for giving. Jesus said more about money than he said about heaven. In a sense we are what we earn. Money represents our time, our energy, our abilities. We express ourselves with our money. Does it all go for kooky clothes, fashionable houses, steak dinners, color television? "For as he thinketh in his heart, so is he" (Proverbs 23:7).

Jesus said we are to render to God what is God's. We are to glorify him by giving what costs us much. He commended the widow who gave two mites because of what that giving expressed of her. He commended giving to support him, as well as giving to the poor. You can find plenty of material on giving just by following Jesus and Paul around.

In the Old Testament God gave firm instructions about what to give for the tabernacle. He also pointed out what to provide for the poor and the stranger. Moses, the spiritual leader, was to declare all these things. God never assumed people would discover the joys of giving without instruction.

The prophets let people know they should be giving. "Bring all the tithes into the storehouse," said Malachi (Malachi 3:10 LB). The Bible gives no hint that God's spiritual leaders are to avoid mention of money. Money is part of life, and life is the pastor's domain. He is to lead his flock.

It goes without saying that the pastor also gives regularly, soberly, in the fear of God himself. Paul says to Timothy, "set the believers an example" (I Timothy 4:12 RSV). To the Corinthians he writes, "Be imitators of me, as I

43

am of Christ" (I Corinthians 11:1 RSV). A pastor can say no less.

Does the financial secretary find the pastor's check among the others? He'd better! If he doesn't, the pastor's words will be sounding brass and tinkling cymbals.

As pastor you say you give your whole life? Your salary isn't big enough that you can give cash? You have to buy stamps and gasoline? We say, hand in the cash. Trust God and the board of trustees for stamps and gasoline.

If giving is good for other people it's good for us too. Before we ask others to take a step of faith, we must take it ourselves. Jesus said, "Give, and it shall be given unto you; good measure, pressed down, and shaken together, and running over, shall men give into your bosom. For with the same measure that ye mete withal it shall be measured to you again" (Luke 6:38).

Giving is for everyone; the pastor leads the way.

Money-Making Projects
—Good or Bad?

"What's wrong with money-raising schemes?" someone asks you. "They're harmless, they keep people busy, and they do bring in a little money. So, why not?"

Of course there's nothing wrong with them—for a club, PTA, or social fraternity.

There's nothing wrong with trying to breathe carbon dioxide instead of air. The only problem is it won't support physical life for humans. Money-raising schemes will not support spiritual life.

In the church they stultify spiritual growth. Anything that stultifies spiritual growth stunts giving. Money-raising by schemes sacrifices long-term for short-term gains. Putting up with them is pennywise and pound foolish.

Hattie Hardwork is a trusting soul. She doesn't know much about trusting Christ. But she does know about trusting her minister. He has asked her to be president of the ladies' aid. Nobody else would take the job. But she feels honored, gratified. She wants to "do the right thing."

She pours out her time and her energy. She believes she's serving a good cause. Her goal? To exceed the $763 produced for the church by her predecessor. She devotes the January women's meeting to dreaming up new ideas for next November's bazaar. Someone brings in a sample of stationery to sell door-to-door or among friends. But is the 50 percent mark-up enough profit for a church group? They debate the matter forty minutes. Someone else suggests a menu for the next church supper. It takes twenty-five minutes to decide whether it shall be ham or something new with hamburger. Whether to charge $2.50 or $2.75 eats up another twenty minutes. The meeting adjourns.

Mrs. Hardwork trudges home to cook for the family. She begins wrestling with the question of whether to have hamburger or ham for supper.

By the end of the year, she feels vaguely cheated. She has worked so hard. All they've come up with is about the same as ever—$771. She tells herself it's selfish to have wanted something out of it for herself. She'll just take a year off from church altogether. Maybe staying away will bring back the old feeling.

Selma Stringsaver keeps a penny-perfect account of her household expenditures. She sews, cans, freezes, shops for bargains. She counts her time spent working on church projects at a modest $2.00 an hour. She adds up time for meetings, setting tables, cooking, crocheting dresser scarves, making aprons. She doesn't omit time spent soliciting merchants for free turkeys or tablecloths.

It all adds up to several hundred dollars a year. That's a lot more than the church ever receives for her efforts, but her husband is proud of her thrift. They don't actually have to give the church anything in cash; she gives her time.

Sylvia Socialite lives in a magnificent home. She has most of her work done, has time on her hands. Fussing over bazaars and rummage sales can fill up her days for weeks on end. These activities provide an excuse for getting out with the girls. She also can spend hours shopping for six handkerchiefs to contribute to the handkerchief booth. Then she can spend a whole day selling the handkerchiefs. Somebody will buy them for $1.00 each, just what she paid for them. She will feel she has contributed $6.00 to the church. The people who buy will feel they have contributed $6.00. The only catch is the church has received only $6.00 —not $12.00.

For Sylvia, church money-raising is primarily a social operation. It also gives her a chance to work with her hands. This she really enjoys and misses in her own home. It's all quite harmless, except that for Sylvia the bazaar is the church.

One Wednesday morning she was leaving the church with a birdcage and three bouquets of artificial flowers. She passed her acquaintance Fran going in to attend Bible class. "Oh, so you're Bible-ing today, are you," she trilled. "Bible-ing" to Sylvia was just another activity like birdcaging and flower-making.

The busyness of money-raising filled up Sylvia's hours in the church. She could dodge any confrontation with the Christ of the universe.

Sally Suburbia garnered for herself an M.A. in biology. She taught in college a few years. Now she lives with her husband and two children in a comfortable suburban home. He teaches economics and struggles toward a Ph.D. degree. She spends her days washing diapers and wiping up spilled milk. The budget doesn't allow for household help.

Recently she decided she needed some outside stimulation. She hired a baby-sitter and managed to get out to a women's meeting in the handsome church she attends. The meeting consisted of instructions on how to make table favors out of matchboxes and toothpicks. Each person was to make one dozen before the next meeting. They wanted six hundred to sell at the bazaar. Sally decided not to go to the next meeting. She decided to take a course at the university instead.

Trying to build a giving church on money-raising schemes doesn't work. It's like trying to drive piles in quicksand. Your efforts will disappear. All the frenzy and furor don't add up to much money. The solicitations and sales lose friends for the church. They fail to influence people for Christ.

The high priest Caiaphas had a good money-raising scheme. He raised animals for temple sacrifices. People had to pay inflated prices for sheep or doves to offer. Of course they could bring their own or buy at bargain rates in local shops. But the priests under Caiaphas always pronounced these animals blemished. Each animal had to have a priest's OK.

Another scheme that brought a lot of income was the money-changing business. Jews from many countries came to the temple during Passover. They had to change their foreign money into Palestinian half shekels for the temple tax. Priests provided this service inside the temple gates—for a fee.

These businesses actually paid. Yet Christ made a whip of ropes and drove them all out of the temple courtyard. He said, "Take these things hence; make not my Father's house an house of merchandise" (John 2:16). They did. Maybe if we listened, he'd say the same thing to us.

Modern churches don't need busywork for either men or women. For entirely too long, churches have seriously underestimated the intelligence of women. Not all women like to work with their hands. Others get more than enough handwork at home.

In our present church many women study in small groups. A class for serious Bible study, with outside preparation, attracts three to four hundred weekly. These women come from our own and many other churches. In the church and outside of it, women serve in many capacities according to their tastes. For those who like to serve with their hands, you can provide worthy outlets. Church fellowship suppers at cost or on a free-will offering basis are still great.

Or women can form a Dorcas society and sew for missions. "All the widows stood beside him weeping, and showing tunics and other garments which Dorcas made while she was with them" (Acts 9:39 RSV).

In our church, thirty to sixty women of all ages meet to sew enthusiastically. They make needed articles for the disadvantaged at home and abroad. While sewing, they stretch their vision and provide a worthy service. They are not under any illusion that they're financing their church by cooking or sewing.

Roadbeds
and Supply Trucks

A supply truck won't get very far if it has no roadbed to travel on. The roadbed which little trucks of sharing run on is commitment to Christ. Armies devote enormous amounts of effort to keeping roads open. Ancient Romans built their roads so solidly that some are still in use. Those roads have deep foundations of large stone blocks. Biblical preaching and education in tithing are roadbeds too. They will take you where you want to go.

Maximillian Moneybags drives up to the church entrance in a floating palace. The make of his car represents the final step up. He lets his wife off. She is clutching her mink in fingers flashing with diamonds. While she waits at the church entrance, the general populace gasp in awe. Each person on the steps debates: Shall I treat her as if she were a human being? Shall I wait for an introduction? Shall I pretend I don't consider her any better than anyone else?

Gertrude Greedy immediately sees the sheen from Mrs. Moneybags' diamonds. She visualizes new carpeting and draperies for the ladies' parlor. Tyrone Treasurer looks at her and sees a dollar sign with four figures behind it. Mr. Moneybags should be good for $6,000 in the campaign for a new addition. After all, he is president of the local peanut butter company.

The minister, fortunately, doesn't see a dollar sign. He sees seeking souls—a man and woman burdened with worries. He knows they are besieged with pleas for money. They hear about needs far greater than those of the local church and have learned to shut their ears to needs. He also knows that wages in the peanut butter business are up, prices are down. Beyond that he knows their only daughter has spurned their values. She has taken off for parts unknown. The minister wants first of all to offer them new values.

Here's an algebraic equation that expresses practically all church giving for individuals, Amount equals commitment in relationship to resources, $A = c/r$ (Amount = commitment/resources).

Lesson number one in church financing: What a

person gives may have nothing to do with what he has. Therefore, learn not even to see what a person has. Giver and nongiver alike have each built up their defense against pocketbook aggressors. Futility is talking about needs of the church to a person with no spiritual commitment. He can sit in the pew figuring the church's needs are your problem, not his. His problem is making the house payments. He also must figure on money for the ski trip next weekend.

Your problem first of all is not teaching him to give. It's helping him to accept a gift. "For God so loved the world, that he gave" (John 3:16). Accepting a gift can be harder than giving. It means admitting insufficiency. It means admitting that peanut butter companies and family diamonds aren't enough. It means opening up to be filled. When we are full ourselves, then nothing we can give is too much. Church needs will become Mr. Moneybags' problem when giving becomes for him an act of worship.

Perhaps your friend Tyrone gives you the word about Mr. Careless. His name is on the church rolls, yet he isn't giving anything. Is there anything you can do about it? Certainly. Go to Mr. Careless, but never mention money. Go to him with the love of Christ. Invite him to come where he can grow in the Word and share in the fellowship. You don't want his money unless you have him. (And, of course, you'll never get it.) Giving is part and parcel with being. The child must first learn to accept his mother's love. Only then can he give love to anyone else. Accepting comes first.

We know what it's like to try to keep clear-eyed under pressure. Those building payments can pummel you. It's frightfully easy to hit back. It was tempting to let the finance chairman stand up and say, "Now if every family would give $150 a year, we would be able to meet our budget." It was what he always had said. But he had to be stopped. Some families on the rolls couldn't even be found. Others couldn't give $150 a year; others wouldn't. Some could and might give $500. But they would automatically trim their giving to $150 if that amount were suggested. Later they'd learn others hadn't met their quota. Then they'd lose their joy of giving altogether.

A church isn't a club with dues. Giving isn't Christian until it's individually tailored in proportion to income "as God hath prospered him" (I Corinthians 16:2).

Even long before Christ, David said, "'I will not offer to the Lord my God whole-offerings that have cost me nothing'" (II Samuel 24:24 NEB). Araunah offered to give that threshing floor for nothing for an altar to David's God. But David refused. He wanted to pay for what he gave.

A husband said to me once, "When I first married my wife, her mother kept buying her clothes for her. I asked her to stop. I wanted to buy my wife's clothes myself." He loved his wife, felt deprived not having the privilege of providing for her. Love has to express itself in giving. We must translate the church's needs into subjective experiences of worship.

But suppose education is moving along as fast as possible. Each member is giving precisely to the degree of his spiritual growth. Yet income still falls short. Don't you have to put on pressure just to get by? No. The only right thing to do at such a time is trim the budget.

Our new program had been in effect a few months. A committee met to budget for the new year. When they wanted to put in a raise for Bart he refused. He knew the money wasn't there. The congregation met to approve the budget. Someone moved to raise the pastor's salary $500 because he needed it. I, who knew better than anyone else that he needed it, opposed the move. Bart shut off further discussion. People were beginning to learn to give, but hadn't learned yet.

A few years later they insisted he accept a raise of 33 1/3 percent in one year. He didn't refuse.

Suppose a man's commitment is great, but his resources are zero. His giving must be zero. Suppose a man's commitment is zero, though his resources are millions. His giving will still be zero. You can't do anything about his resources. Don't even look at them. Your job is his commitment.

Rocks and Rivulets

As Bart faced that congregation, resistance to giving was like an immense rock before him. He had thrown out all their methods of raising money. Responsibility was his to produce the next building payment. He thought of all the immense power of God behind him. Like a flood it could wash over that congregation. But what happens to rocks caught in a flood? That's right—nothing. The flood passes, the rocks are still there.

Yet we have all seen great rocks split gradually by tiny seedlings. And we know each seedling starts with one seed and a few drops of water. We have even seen great rocks worn away by tiny rivulets or by tiny drops of water, if enough fell in the same place. We decided bit by bit was the only way. We hoped to split the resistance drop by drop, seedling by seedling. It would be "precept . . . upon precept; . . . line upon line; here a little and there a little" (Isaiah 28:10).

We both realized no sense of duty or obligation could reach that congregation. The idea of loyalty meant nothing. Pressure made them fold their tents and silently steal away. Status meant nothing to them.

Such appeals had all been tried in the past and found wanting. The appeal had to be spiritual or nothing. These were sturdy, middle-class people. They believed more in the local savings and loan than in the church. As individuals they had a healthy sense of self-preservation. An all out pocketbook attack would never go.

We were quite sure they wouldn't sit still for whole sermons on tithing. Besides, there was so much else they needed spiritually. We didn't want to neglect basic truths of the gospel to talk about money. We had no desire to manipulate by trickery just to get by financially. We wanted to touch wellsprings of action.

Precept upon precept, we decided, would be a bit of education about giving each Sunday. It was only three to five minutes before the offering. I watched that there was never enough at any one time to annoy or bore. Bart watched that there was never a Sunday when it was omitted.

People grew to enjoy the little sermonette. It might be a brief exposition of one of the giving verses. Fresh, little-used ones are scattered all through the Bible. Each one used must be specially selected and studied ahead of time. It's not enough just to spout off one of the old familiars. You can't depend on what pops into your head at the moment.

For example:

And the Lord spake unto Moses, saying, Speak unto the children of Israel, that they bring me an offering: of every man that giveth it willingly with his heart ye shall take my offering. And this is the offering which ye shall take of them; gold, and silver, . . . blue, and purple, and scarlet . . . wood, . . . oil . . . onyx . . . And let them make me a sanctuary; that I may dwell among them (Exodus 25:1-8).

In connection with this verse, Bart might say, "Those who have gone before us have erected this beautiful building. It is our privilege to honor God by giving of our treasure to pay for it. He wants only the gifts of the willing heart. Out of love and gratitude for all he has done for us, we offer a portion back to him."

Can you give to others when you need so much in your church? We believe the answer is yes. In teaching unselfishness, we dare not be selfish. Jesus said, "give to the poor, and thou shalt have treasure in heaven" (Matthew 19:21). God told his people through Moses in regard to the poor:

You shall give to him freely, and your heart shall not be grudging when you give to him; because for this the Lord your God will bless you in all your work and in all that you undertake. For the poor will never cease out of the land; therefore I command you, You shall open wide your hand to your brother, to the needy and to the poor, in the land (Deuteronomy 15:10-11 RSV).

Perhaps times are bad. Some in the congregation are saying they can't give at all. Their income is nonexistent or cut down. Such a time, we feel, is one to emphasize proportionate giving.

For if the readiness is there, it is acceptable according to what a man has, not according to what he has not (II Corinthians 8:12 RSV).

In connection with that verse, Bart might say, "We do not want anyone's worship to be conditional upon his giving. If you have no income, worship without guilt. God wants *you*. But, if you have an income, your income is part of you. God suggests the tithe. We suggest some definite percentage of your income. The important thing is not the church's needs. The important thing is what God means in your life."

Many Bible verses point out that giving must be as wide as the world. We educated in missions from the beginning. At the same time we hoped to get money enough for the building payment. We started a mission program by having missionaries present their work.

Sometimes Bart presented a need or dramatic story from the latest missionary letter. People can easily understand $500 for a pastor in India to buy a motorcycle. He can make many more calls than if he has to go on foot. Knowing what their missionary dollars are going for inspires people to give.

The story before the offering might be a vignette on sacrificial giving. For example:

Recently I called on a widow in our congregation who is shut-in, almost bedridden. She gave me an envelope for the church. She said it was the tithe of her social security, which was all her living. I felt like refusing it.

But I remembered God's attitude toward our giving. He wants none of us deprived of the joy of giving. Paul tells us the Macedonians gave out of affliction and poverty. Their feelings overflowed in a wealth of generosity. "For they gave according to their means, . . . and beyond their means, of their own free will, begging us earnestly for the favor of taking part" (II Corinthians 8:3-4, RSV).

I could not refuse the proffered envelope. I put it into the next Sunday's offering plate. Now is your opportunity to put your gift to God into the offering plate.

You might tell the story of someone who was reached for Christ through a new youth program. Or better yet, the young person himself might tell how he found Christ. As you announce the offering, you could add, "Your giving supports this program for youth."

Some Sundays your "precept upon precept" might be a bit of humor. Humor can often make a point without giving offense.

This week a parent told me a little incident that happened in her family. She gave her seven-year-old two nickels. The child was to use one for candy at the drugstore next door to the church. He was to give the other in Sunday school. The mother wanted to make sure one nickel got into the offering.

After church she asked him, "Did you put your nickel into the offering?"

"Oh, no," he said, "I couldn't. I lost one nickel on the way to church. It was God's nickel I lost, so I bought candy with the one I had."

A story that makes the same point is that of the farmer with ten little pigs. He decided to give one to the Lord. But one pig died—the Lord's pig.

We drew these items about giving from many sources. Bart clipped them from newspapers, magazines, or letters. We found them in books. We watched for them in personal experiences and on vacations. We watched for them in our Bible reading.

61

Stories People Tell

"Lives of great men all remind us
We can make our lives sublime."

Longfellow

We learn most easily by seeing truths incarnate in other people. God knew this. That's why "the Word became flesh and dwelt among us" (John 1:14 RSV). We know what Christianity is because we know Christ.

We, in turn, are to "adorn the doctrine of God" (Titus 2:10) by our actions. Christianity is essentially a giving religion. God gave; he asks us to give. Giving is one way for us to adorn the doctrine.

Editors commission illustrations or photographs to make stories in print more appealing. People are God's illustrations.

Bart used stories of real people in his little sermonettes before the offering. He linked these with abstract principles. Over the months, unbelievable things began to happen. Casual givers became tithers. People who had never given anything had exciting stories to tell. God had supplied their need in unexpected ways when they gave in faith. The congregation had always seemed interested in Bart's little talks about giving. But before long, one of their own got up and said, "This happened to me." When this happened they were electrified.

One of the first to take hold of the new teachings was Paul Pavlinek who was a high school coach. As finance chairman for many years, he had been often discouraged. He can best tell his story himself.

"It was about a year after Bart came to Warren Park. One Sunday, Emily and I came home from church and knelt at the davenport here. We prayed that we would have a real personal relationship with the Lord. At that moment of committing ourselves completely to Christ, we felt he really met us. Ever since, we have known it was a very real experience.

"Shortly after that Bart was urging people to try tithing for a month. He had been talking about proportionate giving—one-half tithe, for example. But at that time he urged us to try tithing for just one month, November.

"We decided to take the Lord on his promise.

However, for us, deciding to tithe wasn't trying it for a month. We pledged ourselves to tithe forever.

"People began to hear that we had decided to do this. Bart asked me to speak at the service. One night I was praying about how I was going to tell it. I looked at the face of Christ that we have hanging in our room. He seemed to smile—it was as if he came alive.

"I described this experience that Sunday. So many people said to me, 'What a wonderful experience you had.' Some asked us to come over to their houses. They wanted to talk about how they could have an experience like ours.

"A dentist invited us over. He questioned us about how they could tithe when they had no regular income. I explained how they could keep track of their income for a month. Then they could give a tenth of that amount for the next month. They did, and I know he and his wife have been tithing ever since.

"Many a time I have sat in people's houses and explained my tithing. I tithe my regular income from the school. I also tithe extra income I make selling cemetery lots. I trust that the Lord will bring in what I need. So many of those people just couldn't understand how it could be done. They couldn't imagine how you could give in such an amount. You have to remember their background, you know.

"About a year after our decision to tithe, a member of our family became seriously ill. Of course we wanted the very best treatment for her. She was three years in one private hospital. Our bills were staggering. Yet all this time we tithed; all this time the Lord provided what was needed.

"Then our family doctor suggested another hospital. He said it was expensive, but he wanted us to try it. It was four times as much as our previous expenses.

"At the hospital they asked how long we could stand the cost. I said one month.

"After one month I was down to nothing, and our patient needed to stay a few more weeks. Miraculously, the next month, enough came in to pay the bills. The head of the cemetery was amazed. 'Everything you touch seems to have turned to gold for you this month. Why?' I told him why.

"All that time our loved one was in the hospital we had one amazing experience after another. For example, one Saturday our money was low. We had just enough to put into our church envelope. But we needed groceries for Sunday. However, we had pledged to tithe, so we put the money into the church envelope. Later that day, the cemetery called and said a man was there asking to buy a cemetery lot from me. I went over.

"It was a man I had been working on for ten years to buy a lot. He was never ready. That day he said to his wife, 'Ma, let's go over and buy something today.' He didn't know what made him decide to come that day.

"Commission from that sale was enough to pay the bills on hand and buy groceries.

"I was willing to sell the house; I was willing to go into debt to pay for needed hospital treatment. But it was never necessary. We had turned over our lives and tithes to the Lord; he provided what we needed through that whole experience.

"Now I don't sell cemetery lots any more. A few who knew me from the past buy from me when they wish to buy before they have to. I have my pension from the high school plus some Social Security to live on. It's not very much, but I taught through the depression years, you know, when salaries weren't large.

"Now we have taken on a number of missionary projects besides our church support. For three years I was called by the Internal Revenue Service. They said it wasn't possible for anyone on my income to give so much. We give twelve to fifteen percent. Finally they told me just to make a note saying I have my canceled checks. They don't call me anymore.

"We've been able to keep this house; we've enjoyed it so much through the years. Besides that we have been able to go to Florida every year where we attend Bible conferences.

"God has certainly proven himself."

What Should I Say?

Once people from the pews were heard from, enthusiasm spread rapidly. Giving became a spiritual adventure. Once a month we asked someone from the congregation to talk. They talked about giving as a spiritual experience, so there was no break from the worship service. We feel they intensify a sense of participation. Only once a year do we ask an officer to report on the budget. The other talks on giving are from a strictly personal point of view.

How do you get people to speak on giving? First, you learn of someone whose giving experience seems worth sharing. What marks a person as an outstanding giver is by no means the dollar amount. It's the way he gives, what he has left after he has given.

Jesus sat down where he could watch the crowds drop money into collection boxes. Some who were rich gave much. When the poor widow dropped in her two pennies he called his disciples to him. He made an object lesson of her. " 'That poor widow has given more than all those rich men put together! For they gave a little of their extra fat, while she gave up her last penny' " (Mark 12:43-44 LB).

There's nothing wrong with making an object lesson of outstanding givers in your church. Usually they are willing to share in a spirit of witnessing. A few days or a week ahead of time, you call someone. You ask him to share his experiences. The usual reaction is shock. Then he asks, "But what should I say?"

Some very definite guidelines you must give him are:

1) Make it personal. Encourage him to talk about himself. Make it very clear that you are not asking for a sermon. You are not even asking him for a little homily or for clever quotations. You can usually give these more effectively than he can. (You should have already shared your own experience in giving.) What does the congregation want to hear from a fellow church member? They want to hear what giving means in his life.

Perhaps he can tell what prompted him to start giving. If giving has deepened his experience of

God, ask him to tell about it. Perhaps some Bible verse has been his lodestar. Perhaps God has tested him in his giving or provided for him in special ways. What satisfactions has he derived from giving? Ask him to share his feelings about giving. This kind of sharing can change lives.

2) Make it short. Tell him he must time his talk. He may say he couldn't possibly think of enough to say to fill up three minutes. The one who says this may go on for twenty-five without knowing it.

Here is what Bill Coniam, a plumber, said when asked to speak before the offering.

"When Dr. Hess asked me to speak, my first reaction was to say, 'No, I'm not a public speaker.' Then I thought my side of things should be heard from. As an hourly worker, a blue-collar man, I should tell what tithing means to me. God has given me the courage to stand up in front of all of you and talk. My wife asked me if I wasn't going to have any notes. I said, 'No, I'll just tell everyone what happened, and I know what happened. I don't need any notes.'

"I just took God at his word. He said, 'Bring ye all the tithes into the storehouse, that there may be meat in mine house, and prove me now herewith, saith the Lord of hosts, if I will not open you the windows of heaven, and pour you out a blessing, that there shall not be room enough to receive it' (Malachi 3:10).

"Several years after I was converted, teaching about tithing sank into my heart. I decided to give it a try. It was not that I was sold on it or understood it. But I figured I wasn't signing any contract, so I could quit any time. But I found that once you start, the blessing is so tremendous you can't quit.

"I have found such serenity comes into your life. Tithing to me is committing yourself to God with your substance. I ceased fearing from day to day. I now know the Lord will provide. I am no longer concerned with being laid off. I know I won't starve to death.

"As a journeyman plumber I work for a master plumber who contracts work. I install the equipment. There is no seniority, your work depends just on your ability. If work slacks up, the master plumber can lay off anyone he wants to. I was laid off only once, for three months. At that time a friend, a bricklayer, offered me a job as a laborer. I took it, glad to get anything.

"Another time I was off for nine weeks on strike. I had no money from the union and of course no unemployment compensation. Still, we kept on tithing what we had. By that time the children were older, my wife had gone to work. Somehow when the bills came, we always had just enough to cover them.

"God has given me so many blessings in my family. He has also given us financial blessings. My income has increased over the years. Also, Betty's income at the bank has increased. We now can afford vacations. We even have some stock in the bank where she works for our retirement.

"We have proved him—and he more than came through."

The Big Givers

Can you really reach the big givers just by education same as anybody else? Don't they need a little special attention? Shouldn't someone call on them to ask for money?

I attended a recent fund-raising dinner for my college which was launching a drive. An expert in fund-raising explained that all but a small percentage of their funds would come from large givers, corporate and individual. Donations from small fry like me were really just token gifts. These were important only because they encouraged the big givers. What they wanted from us at that dinner meeting was names of potential big givers. People on the same giving level would approach them for the college.

That method seems to work for colleges. But we're talking about money in the church. And in the church we have more to do than work that hard at fund raising. We have no paid staff or department to carry through all that machinery, and you'll find you don't need it. You'll be equipped with the sword of the Spirit which is the Word of God. With that you can get to people just with words. Using scripture, line upon line, can pierce the strongest armor. Once inside, there's nothing more for you to do. The Holy Spirit takes over. He can apply the message he wants to each heart.

In our opinion, pressuring potential big givers for the church reeks of criminality. Yet, well-meaning people commit this offense repeatedly in the name of Christ. Our first objection is purely practical—you usually don't get anywhere.

The second reason is more subtle. You may get a gift. But you may get it for any one of a number of false reasons. The big giver's money may be a substitute for giving himself He may give to buy forgiveness for a way of life that leaves Christ out. He may give from habit, from social pressure, for status. He may give from a desire to control.

Only the Holy Spirit can separate joints from marrow, separate the outward from the inward. Only the Holy Spirit can make giving a means of growth. You don't want giving to be a substitute for accepting Christ. "First they gave them-

selves to the Lord and to us by the will of God"
(II Corinthians 8:5 RSV).

Here is the story of a successful businessman.
He hasn't yet been persuaded to speak from the
pulpit, but he's willing to share his experience
anonymously.

"Money-making is my only talent. I can't preach,
I'm not a good speaker. I can't teach. My talents
are very limited. But everybody has something
he can do. I feel what I'm to do for God is give.

"At one time I was very tight-fisted. I made
a lot of money in the construction business then
lost it all. I hit bottom one Christmas in my late
twenties. I didn't go through bankruptcy, but I
was broke. I was scrambling everywhere for
money. I borrowed, put off payments on my car,
barely squeaked through. My wife and I almost
didn't have Christmas that year. Things were
that bad.

"I felt losing all that money was God's way of
straightening me out. He was telling me there was
no use holding onto it all; it was all his anyway.
I told him if I ever made any money again, I'd
give him what belonged to him.

"Now I have four businesses. Out of the profits
I draw a base salary. From this salary I tithe.
Whenever I sell a property or take some profits
out of the business, I give half to the Lord. At
that time I make special gifts. I give to my

church, to Billy Graham, to special projects I'm interested in. I also put some of the money aside in a fund for giving. Then when anything special comes up, I can give without hesitating. If you hestitate, you don't give.

"Beyond the tithe on my salary, I have my own scheme of giving. I don't set any definite proportion of my profits to go to the Lord. In my mind I set a certain amount I hope to give each year. So far I have always been able to give more. Like, at the end of the year, I took $20,000 from profits. I put $10,000 in the bank. I also put a check for $10,000 in the offering plate. It was a special gift for the church building fund.

"Maybe that sounds like a lot, but it's not really. People in my tax bracket are only giving half of what they seem to be giving. Uncle Sam would take 50 percent of it anyway. It isn't like poor people giving who are giving the whole thing. So I don't understand why they don't let go and give it. In my opinion, Christians are too tight-fisted. Ten percent is a minimum to give compared to all God has given us.

"I know you can't keep it absolutely hidden when you give. It gets around. But I try to. I don't want a lot of people approaching me for money. When I give, I don't want it to be because somebody is pressuring me. I want it to be God telling me what to give."

Seeds and Sowing

Education need not be accomplished entirely by the spoken word. You can toss out seeds in printed words—here a little, there a little. Not every seed will sprout, but enough will sprout to make your efforts worthwhile. Sometimes a tract clinches the idea of tithing or proportionate giving. Just one person convinced will pay for a lot of tithing literature.

We put a giving tract in the bulletin about once a month. We often include one when a church letter or the monthly paper is mailed out. If a tract is catchy and clever enough, people will read it.

One charming tract looks something like a valentine. It shows a little girl giving a gift to her grandmother and grandfather. It makes the point that true giving knows no season, requires no reason; it is spontaneous, fresh.

This little folder has many of the qualities to look for in evaluating a tract on giving. Here they are.

1) The tract must be specific. This one deals with one particular aspect of giving—spontaneity. It speaks in specific, personal, pictorial tones. It speaks not in rolling generalities that everyone has heard thousands of times before.

2) A tract must be biblical in principle. This one doesn't quote chapter and verse, but back of it is the feel of Matthew 18:3: "Unless you change your whole outlook and become like little children you will never enter the kingdom of Heaven" (Phillips).

3) It must be appealing and attractive. The layout of one, say red and black printing and illustrations can be very attractive. The shape and the fold look crisp. Good illustrations, color, photographs, design, and stories all help.

4) The tract must not be too long. How much can you read before the service begins or during the offertory? How long are you going to spend on that letter from the church with enclosures? Never assume the reader will be in a mood to sit down and study something. Occasionally this is true, however, if his interest has been aroused. Sometimes he wants definite questions answered.

5) The tract must not be too expensive. You're

sowing these broadcast, not planting one by one.

One attractive tract published by several denominations is a bright red folder with an apple on the cover. Pictures of apples accompany the text inside. It says a man who had nothing was given ten apples. He was to eat three, trade three for shelter, trade three for clothing. He was to give one back to God to show his appreciation for the other nine. But, he decided to eat the tenth one giving only the core back to God.

Another brief and attractive tract is a little gold-colored folder offering a checklist. "Do you measure up to the standards of giving set up in the Bible? Check the following to see if there is anything lacking in you." Eight verses on giving taken from the Bible comprise the checklist.

Another tract in blue and green offers some startling statistics. Americans are fantastically wealthy compared to the rest of the world. "To whom much is given, . . . will much be required" (Luke 12:48 RSV).

This is only a sampling. Many others are remarkably fresh, amusing, interesting. One booklet pictures babies with ridiculously adult expressions over captions on giving. Study that one for its humor. The reader wouldn't need to care anything about tithing to be interested in it. Another gives a chart showing exactly what percentage of your income your weekly giving represents.

Don't limit yourself to your own denomination's

material. It may be insufficient, stodgy, or dull. We find all denominational headquarters are happy to send samples.

Sowing materials on giving is like sowing the gospel. Jesus said the seed might fall on stony, thorny, hard, or good soil. But the sower's responsibility is to sow. Some on good soil will bring forth only thirty- or sixty-fold. But a little of the seed will spring up and bear fruit a hundred-fold.

Our job is sowing.

Do You Dare Preach on Giving?

You don't set out to preach sermons on giving just because you need money. But sometimes you can't avoid the subject. As we built spiritual foundations in one church, we made startling discoveries. Christ preached at least thirty-one sermons on money and giving. That's in the short space of the Gospels. Sometimes Bart preaches through a book of the Bible as a sermon series.

Suppose you are going through Matthew. Can anyone accuse you of harping on money if you just follow the text? You are going along on nice safe subjects like the birth of Christ. The ministry of John the Baptist or the baptism of Jesus cause no pain in the pocketbook. Sermons on Christ's temptation in the wilderness, his call of the first disciples are wonderful. Nobody objects.

You go into the Sermon on the Mount. The

Beatitudes don't necessarily irritate anybody in the billfold. But here's a sleeper, "So let your light shine before people that they may see the good you do and praise your Father in heaven" (Matthew 5:16 Beck).

How are you going to separate the good you do from money in today's world? Too many people are around telling us to "put your money where your mouth is." We don't have a chance to forget that money is coined personality. What you do with money these days expresses you. In that sermon you make various practical applications of the verse to everyday life. Money obviously is one of them. How can anyone say you have gone out of your way to talk about money?

You move on preaching about Christ and the law, Christ and anger. With anger you get into a complicated subject. God doesn't want your gift at the altar as a cover-up for hating your brother. However, Christ doesn't say, "Don't give." He does say, "Leave there thy gift before the altar, . . . go . . . be reconciled . . . then come and offer thy gift" (Matthew 5:24).

Telling us not to give unless sounds like a back-of-the-hand boost for giving. But the boost is there—giving is a privilege for the pure in heart. A tacit assumption is going into those bottommost pilings again. Everybody who is spiritually anybody gives. Christ challenges us to raise our standards till our gift is acceptable.

After that sermon you can have a heyday with adultery, lust in the heart, fornication (Matthew 5:27-32). Nobody's going to admit he doesn't approve of sermons on those subjects. You proceed to deal with swearing, turning the other cheek.

Then . . . wham! It says it in black and white, "Give when you are asked to give; and do not turn your back on a man who wants to borrow" (Matthew 5:42 NEB). A verse like that is like a gall bladder attack. It threatens our whole capitalistic system. It's even out of line with Hinduism. (Hinduism says those who are poor are suffering their just deserts. They sinned in a previous incarnation.) Does Christianity say you are to support every lame duck in the world? What if he hasn't been thrifty, as you have been? Doesn't he deserve to suffer?

Obviously that verse deserves a sermon—and a careful one. On the face of it, it leaves you wide open to villains, sharpers, con men, drunks. Such people misuse all the money they lay their hands on. Does Christ mean what he says?

After this sermon all the little crickets may burst forth in full chorus. They can keep still through sermons on lying, hypocrisy, swearing, and lust. But a sermon on giving may be just too much. You are bringing the world into the church. The preacher is meddling in business, he should stick to spiritual subjects.

If this is the response to such a sermon, don't

stoop to defend yourself. This is the time to be bland, inoffensive. Remember, it's the soft answer that turns away wrath. Just say you were merely taking the scriptures as they came.

"Certainly you, Mr. Blankandrich, have been here for the full series on Matthew. Certainly Jesus covered the full sweep of life. We mustn't skip over any of the precious words of our Savior.

"If I have misinterpreted the plain meaning of this passage, or any other, I'm wrong. Will you please go home and re-read the passage and the references? Then you can ascertain where I have been wrong. My interpretations are only suggestive, not infallible. I believe the Holy Spirit can show you the truth."

And believe it. The Holy Spirit *can* show him the truth. You do not have responsibility to choke the truth down his throat. He is not a horse nor you a veterinarian. You are not obligated to push down a capsule of medicine to make him well.

Assure Mr. Blankandrich of your undying love and affection for him personally. And go right on preaching through Matthew. A few more Sundays will pass before you hit him on giving again. By then he just might have read those passages. Jot down for him the scriptures you referred to in your sermon. Make it easy for him to check on you. You'll need to get him ready for that blockbuster about giving in secret (Matthew 6:1-4). It's there. It gets to people. It knocks out the smugness about gifts that look big but really aren't.

These suggestions are only the beginning of sermons on giving in Matthew alone. In Luke 12:16-21, that rich fool made his million and decided to retire early. He was packing up to move to Florida to start really living. That night he died of a heart attack. He might as well have been giving as he went along.

Preaching through Matthew or another Gospel isn't the only way to run into passages on giving. Suppose you are preaching a series on the Ten Commandments. How can you avoid talking about money in connection with the first? "Thou shalt have no other gods before me" (Exodus 20:3). Or in connection with stealing? Or in regard to coveting?

Or, suppose you are preaching a series of sermons on Christ's parables. In one after another you can't avoid talking about stewardship of time, talents, money. Just give it as it is. People will grow in giving as they grow in other aspects of the Christian life.

It's interesting chugging your way through a book of the Bible. Putting together a train of sermons is fun. You will discover quite a few cars are loaded with material on giving. Simply let scriptures determine the proportion. Hook up the cars as they wait on the sidings.

Is Tithing for Today?

How much should you give to God? Seymour Selfish says, "It doesn't make any difference. Give whatever you please. The church should be glad to receive anything."

Seymour needs some kind of standard, some suggestion as to where to start. Does the Bible offer any? The old question of Malachi strikes into the life of our time as well as his. "Will a man rob God?" Malachi goes on to say, "Bring ye all the tithes into the storehouse" (Malachi 3:8, 10).

Seymour Selfish may say tithing is strictly Old Testament. He may say its use is limited to conditions under law. Now, under grace, he says we have no reason to concern ourselves with tithing. It's an obsolete standard.

Perhaps Seymour's trouble is he likes to toss

green stuff into the offering plate. Round sums like one-, five-, or even ten-dollar bills look and feel so good. He doesn't want to sit down with paper, pencil, and decimal points. His round sums might turn out to be pretty paltry, figured proportionally.

That word "rob" does not refer to hitting a man over the head and running off with his billfold. In the Hebrew it means something more subtle—to defraud. The word means to reach out and claim for ourselves more than belongs to us. We may try to cover up our money instead of showing it to God.

God answers his own question without qualification. "Ye have robbed me." How can a man take anything away from God? Doesn't God live in heaven and we down here on earth with our possessions?

A prosperous American businessman was recalling childhood experiences of tending cattle in Sweden. One day, wishing to be away, he persuaded a sister to do his work. As reward he promised to let her hold a small coin for the day. Money was scarce in that home, so she consented. She worked hard all day and that night returned the coin, well content with her wages.

The businessman related the incident with much glee over his sister's simplicity. But a Christian among his listeners remarked, "Isn't that all you get from your wealth? You hold it to the end of your life then give it up. You have as little as before; the whole of your life is gone." A startled look passed over the man's face. He had never thought of his holdings in that light.

"The earth is the Lord's, and the fulness thereof" (Psalm 24:1). God permits us to hold money in our hands for a while. Then we must give it all back.

We sometimes hear the question, "How much did he leave?" The answer is always, "He left it all."

God has said part of what he lets us have for this life is his. He wants us to give it back to him. In doing so, we recognize that all belongs to him. If we refuse, we are robbing him.

In comfortable insensibility the Jews asked, "Wherein have we robbed thee?"

God answers in specifics, "In tithes and offerings."

Seymour Selfish may say this doesn't apply to him because he can't afford to tithe. He may not realize it, but actually he can't afford not to tithe. Someone has said, "God has been in business longer than you. Adopt his policies, and enjoy security." We can violate God's law in our financial affairs. But we can't expect him to bless them if we do. We become disobedient children, our fellowship with him affected in all areas.

God ordained the tithe long before he gave Moses the law. Some six hundred years before

87

the law, Abraham paid tithes to Melchizedek, king of Salem, later Jerusalem (Genesis 14:17-20). The letter to the Hebrews cites the instance (Hebrews 7:2-6).

Some four hundred years before God gave Moses the law, Jacob slept at Bethel using a stone for a pillow. He had a vision of angels going up and down a heavenly ladder. God struggled with Jacob for supremacy in his life. At last Jacob yielded to God. He promised to tithe all he would possess in the future (Genesis 28:22).

Tithing appears to be an eternal moral obligation. Jesus rebuked the Pharisees for legality in tithing. He said they counted mint leaves in their gardens for tithing, neglected justice, mercy, faith. For this neglect he condemns them. But he doesn't say not to tithe. "These you ought to have done, without neglecting the others" (Matthew 23:23 RSV). Apparently tithing to Jesus was part of the abc's of godly living. We can't imagine Jesus stopping with the tithe. But for some of the rest of us, it's a good place to start.

What Is a Tithe?

We said you don't go out of your way to preach sermons on giving. We will now say you do—sometimes.

For the first several years in that church, Bart scarcely dared mention tithing. Remember, they had no training in giving. Previously, the biggest giver in the church gave $2.00 a week. The finance chairman said everyone talked about what a large sum that was to give.

Bart started out talking about setting aside some proportion of income—2 percent or 3 percent. After a year he felt able to mention 5 percent. After two years he felt he could talk about trying tithing for a month.

To launch this trial period required a special sermon on tithing. He used material we have given in this chapter and the last. A few weeks ahead of time, he began announcing the month for tithing. People whispered and flaunted the question, "What is a tithe?" It seemed an unthinkable amount.

Even people with more biblical sophistication can come up with some sharp questions. Does a businessman tithe everything he owns? Does he tithe his gross income? His net income before taxes? His net income after taxes? Does he tithe his net income after taxes, social security, retirement fund, insurance? After rent or house payments, car payments, grocery, and department store bills are paid? Does he tithe just his surplus?

He had to put simple instructions on how you figure a tithe into that sermon.

A tithe is the tenth that belongs to God. The last chapter of Leviticus explains, "And all the tithe of the land, whether of the seed of the land, or of the fruit of the tree, is the Lord's: it is holy unto the Lord. . . . And concerning the tithe of the herd, or of the flock . . . the tenth shall be holy unto the Lord" (Leviticus 27:30, 32).

Israelites computed their income as the produce of the land, the increase of the flocks, the fruit of the trees.

In today's world a farmer owns, say, two hundred acres of land. At the end of the year he has sold his crop, balanced his books. He lays up seed for next year. He finds he has cleared $8,000. His tithe is one-tenth of his net income or $800. He has probably given part of it through the year. Now he balances his books spiritually by giving the rest.

A salaried man, receiving $10,000 a year, has his social security and income tax deducted. But he has no outlay for fixed or circulating capital as a farmer does. His employer supplies that, amounting to some $5,000 or $6,000 per employee. A salaried man's income is a net income. His tithe on an annual salary of $10,000 would be $1,000. That is approximately $20 a week to the Lord. Like the farmer, he figures his tithe before income taxes and other deductions, not after.

A doctor, or a man owning his own business, is like the farmer. As a self-employed person, he tithes his net income, not his gross.

The Internal Revenue Service calls a minister a self-employed person. (You and I might disagree, but we won't argue that point right now.) As a minister, Bart tithes his gross income—salary plus house allowance, plus car allowance, plus any fees that come his way. We figure our tithe before paying income tax and social security, not after. Perhaps some of these points are debatable. But we'd rather be on the generous than stingy side with God. Certainly that's the way he has always been with us. Beyond the tithe, we give free-will offerings for special blessings or special needs.

Recently someone asked Bart some of these questions about tithing. With this person he refused to get into the whole complicated question. Instead he said, "Just start . . . somewhere."

Some of the most terrible punishments described in the Scriptures came to covetous people. Achan was stoned for taking the Babylonish garment and silver. Gehazi, the servant of Elisha, was stricken with leprosy for his covetousness. Ananias and Sapphira fell down dead in church before Peter. They pretended to give all while keeping some. St. Paul described ". . . covetousness, which is idolatry" (Colossians 3:5 RSV).

The cure for robbing God is simple. Stop it. Give God what belongs to him. "You shall tithe all the yield of your seed, which comes forth from the field year by year. . . . that you may learn to fear the Lord your God always. . . . that the Lord your God may bless you in all the work of your hands that you do" (Deuteronomy 14:22, 23, 29 RSV).

Our obedience to God in money matters brings three results:

1) God's house, the church, and all Christian enterprises are abundantly supported.

2) We prove God true. We discover his promises work in everyday life.

3) God will open the windows, or literally, sluices of heaven (Malachi 3:10). He'll empty out to the last drop all the blessings he has for us. They pile up, overflow. We are not able to receive them all.

How to Conduct
a Pledge Campaign

Last night I called Paul Pavlinek long distance
(see chapter 12). Miles and years dropped away.
Paul and I relived the excitement of seeing that
budget go up from $6,000 to $12,000 to $18,000,
to $27,000. He was financial secretary at the time.

"When we reached $50,000 we just couldn't
imagine it," Paul said. "And when we reached
$75,000 we thought that was the absolute peak.
Before you taught us to give, total Sunday offering
was twenty-five or thirty dollars. Forty dollars on
a Sunday looked really big. The rest of the budget
we got by money-raising schemes and soliciting
outsiders. I can remember going up and down
the business street. I would ask merchant friends
to help us out with our preacher's salary."

I asked Paul about Bart's pledge campaigns.

"There was nothing unique about the techniques," he said. "We had had pledge campaigns before. We always tried to get people to bring in their pledges. But they didn't do it. Furthermore, it got so nobody wanted to go calling to ask for pledges.

"What was different was the spiritual content of the whole program. Bart was asking us for a commitment of our whole lives. Money was only part of it. The unique thing in Bart's ministry was he was always helping people to grow spiritually. He brought in all kinds of things directed toward that end. Tithing is spiritual. You can't reach anybody through tithing who hasn't dedicated his life unconditionally. Tithing alone will never work out. First comes commitment of your life."

Nevertheless, Bart felt he had worked out some pretty good techniques. You can learn about these from any denominational headquarters. Bart felt it took some doing to get hold of these techniques. He collected and compared materials, talked to other ministers, learned by trial and error.

One time he hired a professional money-raising company to run a building campaign. It didn't work out. Their methods cut across his basic spiritual premises. But he watched them carefully, took from their methods what he could use.

Here is what he worked out and used:

1) Choose a particular day, perhaps designated

by the denomination, as every-member canvass Sunday. Focus on having an inspirational service, an appropriate sermon. See that there is a big crowd out to bring pledges voluntarily to the sanctuary.

2) Prepare for the day over a period of six weeks with: (a) letters, (b) calls in the homes, (c) telephone calls on delinquent members, (d) talks before the offering by members of the congregation.

3) Follow up by calling on those who didn't bring pledges to the church.

PREPARATION

Professional money-raisers aim first to stir up interest in all potential donors. In churches, they usually plan a six-week campaign. They may plan a series of dinners. They aim to revive old ties, present the value of the work. They soften up the prospect.

Bart adapted these techniques into practical procedures for our situation. During a six-week period, he concentrated above all on getting people out to church. District leaders called on all members. He visited and telephoned delinquent members, ministered as needed. He never talked about money to any individual. His role to individuals was concern for their spiritual growth and welfare. Education in giving was always for the group as a whole. That way the Holy Spirit could speak in each life as an individual was ready. Bart broke this rule only to answer specific questions of individuals.

During these five Sundays of preparation he did not preach on stewardship. No one mentioned church needs in the services. However, a member spoke before the offering each Sunday for the six weeks. Each of these had a thrilling personal experience in giving to tell about.

In the preparatory period the church sent out a series of three letters. The first aimed to make the benevolence budget live. It told about missionaries we supported, the nature and location of their ministry. Results of their work came alive perhaps by the story of a life changed. Remember, contributors give to people, not to projects.

A second letter gave news about the local mission of the church, the Sunday school, young people's programs, musical or athletic activities. It might point out the value of the church to life of the community.

A third letter asked husband and wife to sit down together, discuss their giving. What proportion of their income could, would, should they give? The letter urged them to share in the inspiration of loyalty Sunday by being present. It warned that any not present would be called on.

Bart did not send out pledge cards. He found

it far more effective for people to fill these out in the service.

CLIMAX

The big day arrived. Members packed the sanctuary. A sense of excitement and participation electrified the atmosphere. Bart aimed to preach an inspiring stewardship sermon.

One of his favorites was the two widows. The Old Testament widow of Zarephath gave Elijah the last of her meal and oil. She believed God's promise that her meal and oil should not fail, till God sent rain (I Kings 17:8-16). The New Testament widow was the one who put into the treasury two copper coins (Luke 21:1-4). Jesus measured her gift not by what she gave, but by what she had left. Both showed commitment to God, absolute trust in his promises.

Another year Bart preached on Galatians 6:7. "Don't be misled; remember that you can't ignore God and get away with it: a man will always reap just the kind of crop he sows!" (LB).

Innumerable sermons for pledge Sunday derive from II Corinthians 8 and 9. Paul wants people to get together an offering for the saints at Jerusalem. He appeals to personal consecration, example of Christ, love of God and fellow Christians. But he's not above appealing to pride, self-interest, competition with other churches. He urges businesslike acceptance of responsibility.

Another time Bart preached on Philippians 4, where Paul thanks the Philippians for supporting him. "Not that I seek the gift; but I seek the fruit which increases to your credit" (Philippians 4:17 RSV). Many of the parables make inspiring sermons on giving.

After the sermon ushers passed out pledge cards. People filled out the cards, having consulted husband or wife at home. Ushers brought the cards up to the altar as an act of worship.

Bart always emphasized that a pledge is not a debt. Trustees sent statements out from time to time. But Bart reminded people that the pledge was an act of faith. It could be revised *up,* as circumstances improved, or *down* as circumstances required. The church never dunned anyone to pay a pledge.

The congregation filed out in the afterglow of an exciting service.

FOLLOW-UP

The financial secretary and a few others always stayed at the church. They ate sandwiches and checked pledge cards against membership. They pushed to get cards ready for callers who reappeared at two o'clock. With cards assigned they relaxed till evening, the fun time.

After the evening service, workers gathered in the pastor's home. It was always a crowded houseful, a time for refreshment and good fellowship. Since Bart and I didn't make any direct contacts for money, we entertained the callers. It was our contribution to the effort.

Pledges from the morning would now have been tabulated. Experience showed two-thirds of the budget would be subscribed at the service. To go over the top really depended on the follow-up. "See the last man" was the instruction for every marginal member. In a training meeting, Bart instructed callers not to press anyone for a pledge. They were not to make a sale. They were simply to ask for an answer. They were to ask that the pledge cards be filled out, handed back in a sealed envelope. The answer could be yes, with the amount, or no.

In the evening gathering, the financial chairman announced total response. We always marveled with humble gratitude that God had moved people to do so much.

Sometimes
the Time Isn't Right

It's very hard to remember bad things along the way. But there's one bad thing we should tell you about. We learned a lot from it.

After about eight years, the original church debt had been reduced, though not eliminated. Yearly income was $70–80,000. Missionary giving had grown from zero to maybe $20,000 per year. Staff increased. We had remodeled an upstairs room into a balcony to accommodate increasing congregations. Two morning services, two Sunday schools utilized facilities to their limit.

But growth had reached a plateau. Later we called it a period of consolidation. At the time Bart felt something had to be done to stir things up. He decided what we needed was a new building. All we had was a sanctuary and fellowship hall. We wanted an educational plant. If the Sunday school could grow, he reasoned, the church would again grow. He wanted to buy a building next door or add a wing to the church.

That church was made up of very thrifty people. They couldn't stand debt in their own lives. They were so happy seeing the church debt being reduced; they couldn't bear to take on another debt.

Bart talked the session into accepting his point of view, overruling sharp difference of opinion. A congregational meeting took place. An elder presented the project of buying the tavern next door for Sunday school space. The owner had agreed to sell for $75,000.

Some in the meeting spoke enthusiastically for the project. Certain businessmen felt the owner was asking what he felt his business was worth. They felt half that amount was all the actual building was worth. Others felt it worth dollars to eliminate his business from our neighborhood. Still others wanted to bypass the tavern, build to our own needs. Others violently opposed taking on any further debt whatsoever.

Someone called for a vote. Of course a majority voted for what the pastor wanted. He got his way.

But they went out of that meeting a divided church. They lined up in factions—those for and those against the minister's project. Few felt any serious need for further space. Present facilities could hold all who were presently coming to Sunday school.

A few weeks went by. The tavern owner held to his price. The vote had authorized trustees to meet his price and buy the tavern.

But they didn't do it. After a few weeks Bart discussed the matter again with the boards. All agreed the proposal had stirred up and bitterly divided the church. In a joint board meeting they prayed. A conviction settled over the meeting that the Holy Spirit was not in the project. Bart saw he had been just pushing it along in his own human strength.

The time was not right. "For everything there is a season, and a time for every matter under heaven: . . . a time to break down, and a time to build up" (Ecclesiastes 3:1, 3 RSV).

Bart decided now was a time for him to break down and drop the matter. He told the congregation the boards had decided not to act at the present time. He and they considered the unity of the congregation more important than any project. The congregation soon forgot the whole question. Peace and joy reigned once again. Rapid growth resumed. We rented the basement of a home across the street for a men's class. I readied the basement of the manse for the intermediate department each Sunday morning. We rented space in a bank a few blocks away for the senior highs.

After a while people realized the Sunday school spread out over the neighborhood. Those thrifty bourgeoisie discovered money was going into rentals for Sunday school classes. Along the way we burned the mortgage of the building in a joyous ceremony. After only two or three years it came from the congregation, "We must build." They pledged the money, built a three-level building of lannonstone. It matched the sanctuary. As soon as builders moved out, the Sunday school moved in filling it up.

The church had moved as a body to back the project. I don't mean there weren't the inevitable two or three dissenters. But there were no factions.

What did we learn? We learned a priceless lesson in the fine art of timing. There may be a right time for a thing. Watch for it. Wait for it. Pray about it. When it comes, seize it.

It eludes the pastor who shoves and pushes to get his way. He just might be wrong. We believe God leads through the Scriptures. We believe he leads through the still small voice of the Holy Spirit. And we also believe he leads through circumstances. Circumstances may be the differing opinions of people on the boards or in the church.

If the church can't move as a body, it may be better not to move at all. We have seen plenty of buildings pastors had imagined would reactivate their churches. It doesn't work that way. Nobody ever came to church because of a building. All too often a minister has to leave a church after a building program.

When a building is actually needed, people see the need. Then *they* put up the building. The spiritual program goes on without a tremor. The pastor need not bog down in blueprints and bricks.

Thirteen years had passed since we started our ministry in that church. The budget reached $110,000. Money was no longer any problem. It was a solid, spiritual church.

One summer evening I walked past the lovely building. I thought with astonishment, "All our dreams for this church have been realized. Now we can relax and enjoy the fruits of our labors."

It's a state of mind God never leaves us in long.

Secret Versus Public Giving

We soon discovered life is not arriving at some goal. Life is asking for strength to work through problems. We moved to Detroit, took on a whole new set of problems. It had been an agonizing departure, like telling your children you were leaving them.

In Detroit, we found ourselves in a situation very good for reducing the ego. A mighty army of dedicated Christians filled the church Sunday by Sunday. Row upon row they looked up eager to be fed. They accepted us lovingly, as God's man and woman for the hour. And they never let us forget that we were not our predecessor and his wife. We lacked certain endearing qualities which they possessed.

Like any congregation, they wanted our strong

points plus theirs combined, all gaps and weaknesses eliminated. Like any others in the ministry, we are earthen vessels.

Our previous church had been on its back when we took it. They were ready for any kind of change. This church was a going concern. Once Bart suggested to an elder that we try changing a detail in serving communion. The elder replied, "Wouldn't it be easier for you to adjust to fifteen hundred people than for fifteen hundred people to adjust to one man?" That settled the matter.

The church had a budget of $168,000, carried a great missionary program. Yet we had dreams for this church, too. We wanted to carry on the ministry in this location and develop a branch church. We wanted to increase the missionary program, perhaps have a radio ministry. More money would have to come in. Funds were always short of needs now.

Ward Church had its own set of mores financially. These seemed fixed as the laws of the Medes and Persians. No mention of money from the pulpit. Giving was secret. "Do not let your left hand know what your right hand is doing" was written into the atmosphere.

Pastor was to preach one stewardship sermon a year. They wanted no year-round education, no pledging. Bart tried having clever tracts on giving folded into the bulletin. Some people shook them out onto the floor disapprovingly.

Members used giving envelopes, but for income tax purposes only. They felt no one but the financial secretary and his assistant should know who gave what. Least of all should the minister know.

It was a remarkable church. They raised $168,000 per year with no more commotion than that. Bart and I felt we should proceed very gingerly with any changes. In opening up seams, he didn't want to rend the fabric. Yet how could he analyze and learn anything? He wanted to learn about giving patterns in this church. How could he when he didn't know anything?

Bart had started out with the notion that a minister should have his head in the clouds. A minister's job, he felt, was dealing with spiritual matters. Others should handle mundane tasks of money-counting.

He became disillusioned with that approach in our first little church. With things going so badly financially back then, he began poking into records. It turned out neither treasurer nor financial secretary was contributing a cent. And they were the only two who ever talked to the congregation about money.

The Bible gives some space to secrecy in giving. But it gives no space whatsoever to hypocrisy. After that discovery, Bart felt it was his duty to know.

In the intervening years, no one had objected

to his knowing—till now. He went back to his Bible to check again. Was it really wrong for him to know?

He discovered Matthew 6:1-4 is concerned with giving to the poor. When the Pharisees were going to give some money to the poor, they would pull out a little silver trumpet. In the synagogue or on the street, they blew it then gave their alms. Thus all would be aware of their good deeds.

If you or I are helping somebody with the rent, we don't proclaim it. If the deacons help out with some groceries, we don't publish names of recipients. Such publicity would humiliate and destroy the recipient. But what about money brought to the church, as an act of worship?

Jesus watched at the treasury to see how they gave. He wasn't checking on amounts. He was studying people. A minister needs to know who's not giving. Why? So he can call on, minister to, help that person to grow. He also needs to know that people handling other people's money are themselves giving.

A woman broke an alabaster box of ointment and poured it on Christ. Christ commended the deed to others present. He said this gift would be forever a memorial to her (Matthew 26:6-13; Mark 14:3-9).

When Cain and Abel brought offerings, their gifts were approved, disapproved, recorded for us (Genesis 4:1-5).

When Israelites gave for the tabernacle, their gifts were noted (Exodus 35:4-29).

Exactly what the woman gave to Elijah is recounted for us (I Kings 17:8-16).

Scripture mentions approvingly Asa's gifts to the house of the Lord (I Kings 15:14, 15).

Giving was public under David (I Chronicles 22, 28, 29).

They set Joash's chest outside the gate of the house of the Lord. People dropped money into it there. Nothing secret about that. (II Chronicles 24:8-10).

The early Christians "brought . . . and laid . . . at the apostles' feet" (Acts 4:34, 35). Nothing private about that either. Ananias and Sapphira were struck dead for hypocrisy, not for giving in public (Acts 4:34–5:11).

Paul certainly wasn't secretive about his collection for the saints at Jerusalem (II Corinthians 8, 9; I Corinthains 16:1, 2). Nor did he keep still about what the Philippians gave to him (Philippians 4).

We believe the matter boils down to motive in giving publicly. Is it for show or for witness? Somebody has said about giving, "Hide when tempted to show, show when tempted to hide."

Bart discussed the matter with the session. He presented what he believed to be the biblical position. They gave permission for him to have a report on the members' giving by categories. In time he was allowed to see the records.

From the report on giving by categories, he learned that a small nucleus of tithers carried the budget of the church. The great mass of members just rode along financially. Many had piously given a dollar a week since the great Depression twenty years before.

Leaders, who were mostly tithers, agreed that education for all was in order. They agreed rationally that more should discover the joys of giving. But emotionally and individually sometimes it was another matter. A few sometimes assured Bart he would ruin the church with his talk about money.

He proceeded with the bit of education before the offering each Sunday. He preached on giving whenever it came naturally into his expository preaching. He distributed tracts on giving, even if some landed on the floor. He shared facts, bad or good, through a statement in the bulletin each month.

He taught them that money in the church didn't have to be a hush-hush matter. It could be talked about spiritually.

A Pledge Campaign
Isn't Necessary

Ward Church taught us something too. They taught us you don't have to have a pledge campaign. Here's the way it happened.

When we accepted the call, Bart asked for permission to develop a branch; they agreed. He knew this would take money; he knew they didn't regularly have an every-member canvass. But they had had a halfhearted pledge campaign for their educational plant recently completed. He didn't think there was anything settled about their attitude.

We moved into the old manse, into the realities of the church. We marveled at the sweetness, spirituality, strength of so many in Ward Church. With plant completed and fully used, the church was at its peak. No more space for expansion existed on that site. The fully built-up neighborhood, the pull of other churches suggested little further growth.

It was too remarkable a church to let bloom in that location alone. We dreamed of two Ward Churches. As we dreamed, Bart studied population movements. People from the church tended to move to a western suburb. We drove about studying locations. If a nucleus of Ward people could be persuaded to start a branch . . .

We picked out a wooded corner, eight acres surrounded by a few houses and miles of empty space. It was a developing area. We looked about, kept coming back to that location. Bart consulted experts in church development. It was an ideal location, and it would cost $65,000. The owner didn't want to sell, even at that price. He preferred holding it for more. Finally he agreed to sell. His conditions? That the property be kept all together and used for a church! At one time he had considered studying for the Lutheran ministry.

God had answered our prayers before we prayed them. "I will answer them before they even call to me" (Isaiah 65:24 LB).

We began holding services in a nearby school. Bart took the matter of the land purchase to a joint meeting of our church boards. Several men knew about real estate appraisals, one bought sites for a chain of variety stores. Both felt the price was too high. Board members batted arguments back and forth. The general reaction was unfavorable. They already had a debt of $125,000. How could Bart expect them to want to go further into debt for a piece of land sixteen miles away?

The church had a history of lack of foresight. When they could have bought a whole block, they bought only a few lots. Later, to put up their educational plant, they had to buy a house and move it off the lot. A cleaning establishment was smack up against another wall of the church.

To get the land, Bart once more had to step out on faith. He said to the boards, "You people don't know me yet, I've been your pastor only four months. But in my ministry I have carried through enterprises requiring considerable faith." He reminded them they had promised us a new manse. Unable to find one that suited us, we had moved into the old one temporarily. It was exceedingly modest.

"Buying this land means so much to me," Bart said, "that Margaret and I want you to take the $30,000 you have laid aside for a manse. We want you to use it for a down payment on these eight acres. Probably we can get a loan from the Board of National Missions for the rest. Then we can have a campaign for pledges to wipe out our total indebtedness. It's not a large debt for a church of this strength . . ."

They were touched by his offer to put the manse money into the land. Though few of them saw the value of the land, they voted to buy. They didn't want to hurt his feelings. But they voted no, absolutely, on any pledge campaign. The no was final. The abortive campaign on their latest addition had been a mistake they felt. They were to trust God for funds.

So the church now had a piece of land that was Bart's project. He had fifty people meeting in a school who might someday want to build on that land. Most were from Ward Church, some were from the neighborhood. "When are you people going to leave and let us have the kind of church we want in this area?" one woman asked. She lived in one of the beautiful homes near the eight wooded acres.

Bart had stepped out on a bridge that might wash away, carrying him with it.

Giving increased with education, but not dramatically. We delved into the church's past to find out why they felt so strongly against pledging. They had been grounded in biblical giving by their first pastor. He had interpreted I Corinthians 16:2 to mean no pledging. "Upon the first day of the week let every one of you lay by him in store, as God hath prospered him, that there be no gatherings when I come." It was a matter of conviction as well as custom and usage.

Regretfully, Bart laid away all his carefully worked-out plans for securing pledges. He mumbled and groaned—to me, of course. He deplored this unbusinesslike, haphazard, muddling-through method of financing a church. He felt he never knew where things stood.

But income swelled that first summer to meet payments on the land. For the first time the church went through the summer in the black. The boards were amazed. They decided they had done the right thing in buying the land. Two years later they were offered more than twice for it what they had paid.

Sometimes things looked difficult. "The Lord will provide," the elders told Bart and went right on calmly worshipping, praying, working.

Bart believed in faith, too. But this sort of thing made him a little nervous. He watched the peaks and swoons in giving with some anxiety.

It was one church, in two locations. We put up two building units on the eight acres. We had an assistant pastor in the city church, one in the branch. Sunday mornings Bart preached at both.

Strangely, as the years rolled by, we discovered money came in to pay all bills. The church rumbled along. As a new building went up, enormous bills for construction came in. Bart shared the needs. Giving miraculously expanded to cover needs.

Sometimes there were crises. One was when the chapel cost $30,000 extra because of underground water. The architect had failed to take borings. It was a time to panic. But years before Bart had discovered a basic attitude. He laid the problem before the church family. "I trust God and trust you to meet this need."

This attitude always seemed to move people to give. The need always had been met. They gave money to meet this need. Construction could go on. Overall giving increased tremendously—from $168,000 to $335,000 for the two churches. Bart began to say it was a relief to be rid of all that machinery of money-raising. He never had to face the pressure of a financial campaign. He could concentrate on preaching and personal ministry.

We had to conclude that the key factor in increased giving was not the machinery. The slick procedures—the big build-up and thorough follow-up—were not of prime importance. In our experience, the key factors were rather:

1) A biblical basis for giving, emphasizing tithing and proportionate giving. Of course this means eliminating money-raising schemes.

2) Education Sunday by Sunday, spacing it according to what people will take. If you get complaints of too much talk about money, drop it for a few Sundays. Perhaps have someone talk before the offering about another aspect of the Christian life; he might share an experience of witnessing or serving in church or community. Then you can come back to the subject of giving. You will learn to weigh more heavily complaints from a giver than from a nongiver. The latter's

annoyance may mean only that education is getting to him.

3) Sharing the facts whether good or bad. Church members, like a family, respond to knowing.

The time came when the city church wanted to shuck off its child. Bart had to make a choice. The child seemed to need him most. It was a friendly division, a growing up.

Ward Church, Livonia, started out with a building debt of $158,000 and half of the missionary load. Their annual income had gone from zero to $153,000 in twelve years.

They follow the pattern of Ward Church, Detroit. Old members proudly tell neighbors and friends there's no pledging. New members are amazed that no one ever approaches them individually for money. Neither pastor nor people have any desire to go back to pledging.

Ground-Breaking

(Certain special occasions cry out for solid instruction or inspiration on giving. Launching a building program is such a time. Several years ago we turned the first shovelful of dirt for a needed sanctuary. Bart tells the story of that ground-breaking day):

Almost every minister at one time or another builds an addition, redecorates, puts in a basement. Or he builds a cathedral. At such times there is always someone to say, "Why spend the money?" I feel it's best to gather up answers into a resounding sermon. The best defense is a good offense.

Actually I had no desire to build another building. Yet it was needed. More than a thousand people a Sunday worshiped in a chapel designed for three hundred. The crush between services, the overflow in the basement were turning people away. A man of great faith was positive God wanted a sanctuary here. He took it upon himself to bulldoze through all obstacles to get a sanctuary under way. The amount of money we had to borrow appalled me. But Harold Haddon had worked out projections. He swept the church—and me—along with him. To him, worshipers must have a place in which to worship.

On ground-breaking day I based my sermon on I Chronicles 28 and 29. It went something like this:

"Building, altering, adding on any scale is always a big project. Before dream becomes reality, leaders must catch the vision. An architect must prepare plans. Builders must gather materials. People of the church must cooperate to make it all possible.

"We are undertaking to build a sanctuary. How many people will come to know Jesus Christ here, God alone knows. We can't foresee how long it will last, how many generations will worship here. The temple David prepared for and Solomon built lasted over three centuries. Some cathedrals of Europe, even chapels, have lasted longer than that. Margaret and I visited a small Norwegian church a few summers ago. It had been used for five centuries or more."

I went on to talk about preparation (1) of the leadership, (2) of the plans, (3) of the materials, and (4) of the people.

1) "David the king was relaxing in his beautiful new palace. It struck him God's tabernacle was a flimsy tent; he dwelt in a house of cedar. He resolved to build a house for God better than his palace. Filipino Christians out in the barrios worship in huts of nipa leaves. They feel these are quite adequate as places to worship God. They live in nipa huts. These are cool, charming, suited to the climate.

"You and I live in houses of brick, stone, wood. Wouldn't it belittle God to say the cheapest building possible was good enough for him? Shouldn't the church where we worship be in keeping with the houses we live in?

"David assembled at Jerusalem leaders of the nation. He stood and said to them, '. . . My brothers and my people! It was my desire to build a temple in which the Ark of the Covenant of the Lord could rest—a place for our God to live in. I have now collected everything that is necessary for the building' (I Chronicles 28:2 LB). But God told David he was not to build; he was only to prepare for his son Solomon to do so. Great numbers of people have never realized their own desires in life. They have, however, prepared for children or successors to realize those desires. The important thing is God's timing, not ours.

"David said, 'God . . . chose me . . . he hath chosen Solomon . . . to build an house for the sanctuary' (I Chronicles 28:4-10).

"As we embark on a building project, we need the assurance David gave to Solomon: ' . . . Be strong and of good courage, and do it. Fear not, be not dismayed; for the Lord God, even my God, is with you. He will not fail you or forsake you, until all the work for the service of the house of the Lord is finished' (I Chronicles 28:20 RSV).

"David reminded Solomon of those at his command: Priests and Levites, every man with skill, officers, and all people would work. As members of the church, we must all contribute our efforts to our great undertaking.

2) "Every project has to have a plan. God gave David plans for the temple: 'All this he [David] made clear by the writing from the hand of the Lord concerning it, all the work to be done according to the plan' (I Chronicles 28:19 RSV). God gives to architects and engineers ability to prepare patterns for construction. He gave Moses minute details for making the tabernacle."

We were soon to go out and put a shovel into

bare ground. To those people in the crowded chapel I said:

"Many chapters in Exodus demonstrate that God is interested in such details. Plans and specifications for our building have been worked out. Architect and committee have planned for sanctuary, offices, classrooms, and choir rooms. Today we break ground, tomorrow the construction company moves in. Stone masons, bricklayers, plumbers, electricians, carpenters all will follow the architect's plans.

"Sometimes plans aren't followed. When a church I formerly served was under construction, stonemasons built a wall out of line. The architect, Hugo Haeuser, made workers tear down a lannonstone wall and build it plumb. Plans make for safety, symmetry, harmony. What if workers followed their own ideas without regard to one another? Each of us needs to build our lives into the eternal structure of the Church.

3) "Many pages of the Old Testament are taken up with gathering materials for the temple. Millions of dollars in gold, silver, precious stones, marble, and wood made the temple possible.

"David did not try to skimp on the house of God. He and the people provided gold where gold was required. They used silver where God had specified silver. They furnished precious stones to use where the plan called for precious stones.

"David did not say, 'Gold costs too much. I shall use copper or brass. God will never know the difference.' Today, many people give pennies when they should give dollars. They give dollars in singles when they should give in hundreds. Too many people went off the gold standard long ago in giving to God. When God asks for a tithe they substitute a pittance; then they wonder why they have no great joy in their Christian lives. You can rob God if you choose to. He will not send a bill, or a collection agent, or a police officer. But you pay in other ways.

4) "Most important of all was preparation of the people. Hearts and purses responded to the example of leaders. David set an example in giving goods as well as in expending energy. 'And now because of my devotion to the Temple of God, I am giving all of my own private treasures to aid in the construction. This is in addition to the building materials I have already collected' (I Chronicles 29:3 LB).

"He challenged people to follow his example: 'Who will give himself and all that he has to the Lord?' (I Chronicles 29:5 LB).

"Wonderful response came forth that day. Princes, captains, rulers, leaders stepped forward. Each gave according to his wealth. Everyone was excited and happy for this opportunity of service.

"David was overwhelmed with the joy of giving.

'but who am I and who are my people that we should be permitted to give anything to you? Everything we have has come from you, and we only give you what is yours already!' (I Chronicles 29:14 LB).

"Then all bowed low before the Lord. They offered burnt offerings, feasted, drank before the Lord with great joy.

"They gave of what God had given them. They shared in the eternal purposes of God. We too can have that glorious experience."

I quoted from a missionary to Indonesia.

"'After I had finished speaking at Pangkalpinang, there were announcements. The building committee for the new church reported that all money was used up, and they asked what they should do next.

"'Two men took gold rings off their fingers and gave them as a contribution; they had no ready cash. Others gave gifts of money so the work could go on another week. One of the elders got up to speak. At first he could only stand before us and weep. Soon he managed to speak. He said he was weeping because he saw the brethren taking off their rings. He knew how much they prized those rings. When they put them into the collection he knew the Lord was still with them. The gifts melted his heart.'"

Speaking to my congregation about our building I said:

"More important than our building of brick and mortar is what our giving represents of us. It demonstrates tangibly that we are a committed fellowship of believers. We love the Lord and love each other. We want to send our witness through the Detroit area and throughout the world."

Then we sang a hymn, filed out for the ground-breaking. Such a day, in our day as well as David's, can be a love feast of joy and common purpose. It was one of my most effective sermons.

You don't need to be afraid to preach on giving.

Epilogue

We're in the new sanctuary now. Harold Haddon's projections were right. It's filled once every Sunday morning, partially filled for a second service. And there's money to pay for it. In four years, giving has increased from $153,000 to $494,000 per year.

We have increased our missionary budget. Among other projects we support a man and his wife working full time in our inner city.

Where does all that money come from? We marvel ourselves. It's not a congregation of wealthy people. It's a congregation of people who in varying degrees are committed to Jesus Christ. They give as God has blessed them. They want to do their part to see God's kingdom extended on earth.

"Like a mighty army moves the church of God." If dollars are coming in, then bills are paid, boards are happy, new projects can be undertaken.

Once we worried about paying a $390 coal bill in a budget of $4,000. Perhaps it seems like a long way to come. It's not really. It has all come just one tiny little step at a time. Everything we now know we learned just one thing at a time.

What we are trying to give you is not a mold into which any congregation can be poured. It's a set of biblical principles to be adapted to your situation. Just open yourself up, and ask God to show you. Then pick the brains of all who come your way who might help you. We've found God sends along people and books to teach us lessons he wants us to learn. We pray this book will help you.

Keep loose. Keep flexible. We are still learning.

Start . . . where you are.